WILD LIAR

Books by Deborah Pope

Fanatic Heart
Mortal World
Falling Out of the Sky
Take Nothing
Wild Liar

WILD LIAR

Deborah Pope

Carnegie Mellon University Press
Pittsburgh 2023

Acknowledgments

Thank you to the editors of the following journals in which some of these poems first appeared:

Birmingham Poetry Review: "Sometimes a Voice"
The Café Review: "Lifelines"
Cave Wall: "Waning Crescent," "Notes for My Eulogy"
Cider Press Review: "Formal Family Portraits"
Hampton-Sydney Review: "Fragment"
Plainsongs: "Remainder," "Solitaire"
Poetry East: "Vows"
storySouth: "An Evening at the Angus Barn"
Tar River Poetry: "The Old Fathers," "Photograph of a Girl"

Book design by Mary Warner

Library of Congress Control Number 2022943774
ISBN 978-0-88748-689-0
Printed and bound in the United States of America

10 9 8 7 6 5 4 3 2 1

for Dean

Contents

III

I

Sometimes a Voice

is alive as dice in the fist, quick as a kid
on a hot slide, sure as salvation in the blues,
is cash on the barrelhead, corn on the cob,
pie in the sky, the real deal, all in, last call,
good as gold, doesn't wait to be told,
is bless your heart and bold as brass,
knows highways, beltways, one ways, subways,
cafes, diners, dives, corner bars, coffee bars,
window bars, tar stink, diesel stink, river stink,
hot stink of chain link, knows midtown,
uptown, downtown, underground, small towns,
hometowns, throw downs, has been around,
is bearing down, homing in, knows upbeat,
back streets, gravel roads, dust roads, no roads,
knows depots, silos, closed signs, coal mines,
legion halls, local granges, shift changes,
church dinners, lawn spinners, saints and sinners,
won't bide its time, toe the line or know its place,
won't wait in line, crosses the line, plays it
nervy as a jazz line, lines it up, calls
eight ball in the side pocket,
as good as its word.

Introduction to Poetry

Let's start with the trouble with poems.
The trouble is we want them to be clear,
concise, and to end with a click as tight
as the clasp of a coin purse, to slip as easily
into our minds as a stopper into a wineskin.
We want them to deliver on cue—
the no-haggle deal we drive right off the lot,
the hanging fastball straight across the numbers.
We want to be noticed, not watched,
with a route through a poem like a city bus
where we know all the stops and when to get off.
But poems aren't precise as a fixed-price meal,
consumable as a blue-ribbon pie at a picnic
and disposable as a paper plate. They won't
break open like a fortune cookie with a message
as bland inside. They'll ditch the interstate
for hairpins down the Devil's Backbone.
They won't dance to our tune. They sway
to their own music, like a woman balancing
a basket with clothes pounded clean in a river.
The trouble with poems is they don't care
what we want. They climb in our windows,
throw open the doors. They disclose, disarm
or warn as they please. Some ferry across
waters so dark, so deep, their freight is
still reaching us as rumors.

The Art of Losing Power

after Elizabeth Bishop

Snow is blowing sideways at the angle
of a child's slide, coming down like dots
from a paper punch, glazing the ground
like icing on a cake. The wind seems intent
on bending the pines and the power just went.
We lose water, lose heat, but there's a woodstove
and out on the porch you're mastering the art
of the camping stove with its tidy, blue bracelets
of flame. We sip tea, burn candles, content
in our blankets. It's almost a lark. It's no disaster.
We're not flustered losing track of hours spent,
mustering up soup, crackers, honey—enjoying
how time goes slower, not faster. A little calamity
is meant to flatter our patience, resilience,
the subtle deceits that let us believe crisis
can be mastered. But if it turns vaster—
trees snapped, food down to the last or
houses lost to dark for days—still it would
seem something we should have seen coming,
have better prepared for, unlike real disaster
that hits blind, hits fast, hits even after
it's evident how terrified and helpless we are,
lying there, where the world will never
right itself again—like me if I lost you.

The Question

A famous poet once said
that all our life we are speaking
one long sentence, from our
earliest words to our last.
If so, I think that sentence
must be a question, one
that is our life's journey
to answer. Perhaps it takes
years to even learn what
our question is. Or we might
spend our lives pursuing a question
that is not, in the end, ours.
Or the answer may be one
we do not recognize
or believe. Yet all of it—
the knowing or not knowing,
the finding or not finding—
becomes our story.
Maybe love is simply finding
someone whose question is ours,
or hate arises from denying
the questions of others,
of failing to see the beauty
and the pity of them.
Perhaps, who knows,
the questions will finally be
those we ask from the start—
Who will keep me safe?
Have I been good?
How much farther?
When is the end of
If only?
What now?

Fragment

There was something I meant to tell you.
It would have explained everything.

But I cannot remember it now.
It was something of the past,

of how it happened with you, with me,
with us—all those turnings, choices

and consequences, what we got right,
what we got wrong, and how it all

might have been different, easier.
Maybe it came in a dream that frayed

on waking, or a moment's clearing
in the mind, hovering just there

on the periphery of memory,
or like the system of a great river

seen for an instant from above—
its veins and tributaries forked and moving

to their inevitable confluence—
before the view closes, blurs into

a distance invisible, inexpressible—
so that now I cannot bring it back.

Believe me, always I loved you.
But then I told you that.

Remainder

There comes a time when,
as if you have never thought
of it before, suddenly you see
the years ahead are fewer
than the years behind,
fewer days, fewer hours,
fewer springs, falls, less,
you realize, of everything,
and against all your wanting,
wanting not to, you begin
to subtract the age you are
from some age that waits
and you look at that sum—
and whatever you do now,
whatever it is, you will think
there is something more,
something else,
something other
you should be doing.

Memory for Beginners

Memory, like every liar, says,
"I will tell you the truth."
It tells you the past will be there,
intact, retrievable.
Is anything ever that simple?

                    *

Memory is messy, grainy, eludes
the cagiest net. It is pattern
and disruption of pattern,
a composite, a palimpsest,
a threshold into warrens
of branching rooms.

There are no flawless simulations.
Nothing is ever again as it was at the start.
Something is always missing,
by mistake or design.

What was vacant returns full of meaning.
Emotions come out of hiding.
Someone unremembered
returns, or you remember
what no one else does at all.

                    *

All the lost people and times of memory,
the remnant, the disappeared—
like a child's game of musical chairs,

except when the music stops
it is the child, not the chair, that is gone.

*

Pitted against memory,
accuracy is meaningless.
There is the past as it was
and the past as you remember it was.

Lover and lover, father and son,
sister and sister, at the mercy of
each other's memories, insisting
it was one way and not another.

*

Who is the you? Who is the I?
Who the observer, the observed?
Why this? Why now?

*

The endless deciphering.
What can stay in place against it?

*

The arc of memory is revision.
Details recede. Invention enters.
Memory becomes story,
story becomes memory.

The photograph in the frame becomes
the photograph in the mind.

*

Given time, only the telling remains.
The rest runs away.

Given time, memory is a wild liar.

Winter Solstice

I

A seer says to me,
In the right pocket of every journey
is a question. In the left, is a gift.
I ask, *What is my journey?*
What is my question? What gift do I have?
But I do as I'm told. And wait.
Nothing comes. No one answers.

II

Then a door in my mind opens.
I am a peasant girl in torn sheath
riding the back of a great, white bear,
traveling on a midnight plain.
Lights of the aurora borealis flare high
on the horizon. They seem to guard
the end of the world. Out of their shadows
the shape of an ice-angel comes.
Icicles, star points, spike and shine
from her hood of fur.
I ask for a gift:
she gives me words.

Without sound or touch, I feel them drifting
and swirling like snow in the night.
I ask if my journey is done now.
Behind her the sky fires point
their great crooked fingers.
She raises her shaggy sleeves and hands me
a cloak pricked with stars from a new moon.

I understand I am to wear it to travel the dark
unseen, unknown. Emboldened,
I ask for more.
But the bear has gone.
The horizon has closed its bright box.
Even the wind pulls away from me.
I know there is to be nothing.

III

Time has either passed or stopped.
Then another woman approaches.
She says she will take me to the circle
of three fires. Wrapped in my cloak,
I visit at her bidding the fire of work.
The fire is strong, globed with heat
and steady flame. I reach my hands
toward it, letting the palettes of gold
and garnet warm me through.
I want to stay here.

Instead I am sent back into the dark
to find the fire of family.
But there is no flame, only coals
burning blood-red under the ashes.
They smolder and break.
A deceptive fire. It could silently,
suddenly, kindle, catch, leap up
without warning. It could also
go out altogether. It needs constant watching.
I waver, anxious, not knowing
if I have anything to give it.

Before I can learn, I am told to move on
to the fire of connection.
But in the place where I was to find it,
nothing is yet made.
I see only a box of matches.

IV

Then my mind closes, the spell unwinds
to an ordinary house by a lake in December.
My spine has gone stiff and everywhere
I am cold, restless, thinking this way
of searching, proceeding, is too hard
and requires a courage and credulity
I am not sure I possess. I wanted
the questions, the gifts, the fires,
to do my work for me, to smooth my path.

Instead I have returned to a road
of uncertain choosing with tools
that seem too common and poor
for anything—some words,
some matches,
a cloak of dreams.

Lifelines

An expert told me that I have six planets
and four angles in my Ninth House,
that my familiar is a bear and that I will create
a great work late in life. I have also been told
the lifeline in my palm is forked and my heart
line is broken. And a woman I knew could
recount her past lives in impressive detail.
She'd been male and female, child and crone,
a Sufi, an Aztec, a nun in the time of Assisi,
though in what order she did not say.
I could almost believe my children were cats
or barbarians, my gentle husband once my mother.
I would like to have been a woman with a lute,
a weaver of sagas, or a girl who saw visions
in the fire, each existence a curious bead
in an abacus of mysterious tallies, and I regret
I know no other lives than this one.

For doesn't something in all of us long to be
more than one character, to have more than one
story to tell? Who wouldn't want to appeal to
some Mender of Destinies to let us step up on
the cosmic scale and spin an arrow of options,
especially if it could be weighted in our favor.
We might stop in the slot of a life where scores
are settled, debts are paid, our virtue rewarded.
Or is our desire simply to believe we can go on
speaking in some infinite, elastic theater of time,
keep our voice going, our words pushing back
with each spin against silence? Won't that be
the hardest part when life comes to its end
and leaves so much still to explain, forgive?
Can any one life ever finish it?

The Old Fathers

The old fathers are disappearing.
They left the gardens turned,
the tomatoes tied. They left
twine, penknives and handkerchiefs
in the soft nest of their pockets.
They left seed spreaders
and sprinklers of half-light
summer evenings stored away
with storm windows, tackle boxes
and peach baskets. They turned
off the yellow porch lights,
adjusted thermostats,
wound the tall case clocks,
emptied their loose change
in small dishes on dressers
and entered into their journeys
of moonlight and shadow,
the dogs long since whistled home.

Confessions of a Failed Theologian

I do not know, as old theologians debated,
how many angels can dance
on the head of a pin, or if they can
extend in space, as Aquinas believed.
He also said that angels reside in
ranks and hierarchies, from Thrones
and Dominions to the highest reaches
of Cherubim and Seraphim, from whence
they descend like celestial troubleshooters,
intermediaries, whereas souls seem
always to reside with the human.

I do not know how much the soul weighs
or whether it is hard or soft like the heart,
though some have sought to extrapolate this.
And I do not know if for each body
a soul is created, or if the body creates
the soul, like a second skin it slips into.
Or is the soul always floating just above,
like a weather, not trapped in
the insistent, sweating moil
of the body corruptible?
Are souls a lottery or a bazaar?
What one is given or what one bargains for?

When we die, does the soul mourn for us,
or is it gladdened to be free?
I like to imagine souls go to a great,
echoing station fuming with stone and mists,
where they wait by equally great tracks
reaching out of sight. Without schedule
or timetable, trains stop, open,

a soul steps in. But to where? To what?
Do angels chivvy them along?

It could be that some are gathered up
and redeemed like a coupon or ticket.
Or they are thrust into a new body
to be born, to become better,
until burnished at last.
Or they simply go, each by each,
into the hands of their own belief.

I know there are people with answers.
They will call down prophets.
They will show me books.
The prophets and the books will quarrel.
So I do not know if light is better
than darkness for knowing.
And I haven't mentioned the tripwire
of grace, but there must be
room for it somewhere,
however fugitive, improbable.
Maybe it is not the number of angels
on the pin that matters,
but that they are dancing.

The Duties of Saints

St. Barbara, of the Fourteen Holy Helpers,
lived in a tower, dining only on honeysuckle
and locusts. For adding three windows,
she became the patron of architects.
Because her tormentors were struck down
by lightning from the heavens, she would
henceforth favor all manner of munitions,
miners and fireworks.

In recognition of St. Lawrence's quip
to "turn me over, I'm done on this side,"
while being roasted on a griddle,
he has been given particular care
of comedians, clowns and chefs.

But pity St. Clare of Assisi, founder of
the Poor Clares, an order devoted
to silence. But because she witnessed
the Mass in vivid colors on the wall
of her cell, she must now endure
as the patron saint of television.

Archangel Gabriel, as the Messenger,
takes broadcasters and mass media
under his wing, while St. Bernardine,
who, when hoarse from preaching,
had his voice restored by a megaphone
of miraculous fire, intercedes
as the patron of advertising. May he confer
with Sts. Felix and Pancras, who descend
to confound false witness.

Students, assisted by Sts. Brigid and Aquinas,
congregate in coffeehouses which fall
within the purview of St. Drogo.
There they are served by baristas
under the aegis of St. Martha,
also patron of waiters and dieticians
for her work preparing food for her Lord.

And in that air, redolent as a censer
with the aroma of Arabica and Peru,
others also hunch, as if in solitary prayer,
over computers protected by St. Isidore,
Schoolmaster of the Middle Ages.
For his prodigious output of chronicles,
histories and ephemera, his duties also
extend to the internet.

However he is spared its hackers.
These are assigned to St. Columba,
the warrior saint, who stole St. Finnian's
Psalter, covertly copying it by writing
in the dark with only the burning fingers
of his left hand for light.

How serene, then, and lofty must seem
the realms and hours of St. David,
who has only doves, Wales and poets
in his tending, though as to the last,
their numbers are legion and, when not
exultant, are known to be so brooding,
unruly and importuning a rabble
as to try the sufferance and patience
of even a saint.

Notes for My Eulogy

I admit I did not read the instructions first.
I did not separate my colors.
I spoke before I was spoken to
and did not think twice.
I did not know what was good for me.
I did not carry a big stick
or keep my enemies closer.
I never gave the Devil his due.
I put all my eggs in one basket and did not sell high.
I couldn't leave well enough alone.
I did not leave my worries on the doorstep
or smile, smile, smile.
I did not see the error of my ways.
I did disturb.

It's true I did not get my motor runnin'
or head out on the highway.
I did not keep on truckin'
or go hear Uncle John's band.
I let wild horses drag me away.
I did not stop in the name of love.
I kept the old records on the shelf.
I was not wonderful tonight.
I could not look at clouds from both sides.
The times were not changing enough.
I knew much about history.
I could not let it be.

I confess I only looked eight ways at a blackbird.
I had a mind of summer
and thought April was a tender month.
I did not always go when the evening was spread out against the sky.

29

I took the well-traveled road
and had to stop for Death.
I remembered what lips my lips had kissed.
I practiced, but was bad at losing.
Truth was only rarely beautiful.
I did not hear America singing.
I could tell the dancer from the dance.

But I imagined and it was easy if I tried.
I dwelled in possibility
and got the news from poems.
I gave glory for dappled things
and petals on a wet, black bough.
I considered the lilies
and how my light was spent.
I had promises to keep.
I knew a man, lovely in his bones,
who loved my pilgrim soul.
We had world enough and time
and peace came dropping slow.
Just say I was a lucky so-and-so.

Winter Rain

And still it comes on,
the sound and pound
of it drilling the roof
with a pocking of drops
pinging up from the tin
like mercury pop beads
and falling in silver
chains from the rim,
rivering and racing
in veins on the glass,
runncling the lawns,
pummeling the gulleys,
hastening our hours
into dusk, the dusk
into dark and the black
wash of sleep where
water is our element,
coursing through dreams
where our lids float up,
we grow gills, become
primitive things with
primitive longings,
taste river, taste salt,
taste ocean, sinking
and rising in the lung
of the surf, the trough
of the waves and the pull
of an aqueous moon
hauling us back to
the sodden world
again, surfacing
breathless.

Vows

I love you the way a coin
loves a slot,
the way an arc
loves its limit,
the way a changeling
loves the forest.
I love you the way dice
love a chance,
the way a spiral
loves a tower
the way winter
loves the moon.
I love you the way music
loves silence,
the way glass
loves water,
the way a map
loves horizons.
I love you the way mercy
loves mystery,
the way stories
love beginnings,
and how one footstep
loves another,
and another.

Waning Crescent

Tonight the moon is a thin, white wire
curved like the indentation when a hammer
just misses a nail. Its dimming makes
the span of stars so bright they almost
seem a summoning. Beneath them an owl
flies out low and close from the forest,
a brief flare of fixity and flight.

I think of time, not its illusion of fixity
and flight, of arrow and horizon,
but of time as it is—a circumference,
a circle we continuously move within,
a coil that slowly winds and tightens itself.
And of memory, time's mirror, like a great
upsweeping of birds that scatter and gather,
scatter and gather, forever forming
and breaking form, a winding skein
in patterns of incident and inference,
shadow and dream.

If I could hold one pattern back
it would be the day just passing,
with the fires of nasturtiums,
like blown-back umbrellas, balancing
on their lily-pad leaves, and the sons
and daughters of sons running
in the young sling of their bones,
following the stuttering flight of a skimmer,
their lives in the harbor of hands
that still hold theirs, and the woods beyond,
with their hundred shades of green
and leaf-light turning into the beautiful

glooms of the forest before circling
into this night, this hour, the stars
revolving on their luminous wheels.

Daphne in Arcadia

Imagine what she feels,
turning to wood—the soft flesh
twisting and fusing to bark,
arms stiffening in branches,
her once swift feet forking
to roots, the hardening throat
sealing up forever. What form
of rescue, of escape, is this
for the frightened girl fleeing
Apollo's panting pursuit?
What answer from her father,
the river god she prayed to
to save her? Did he smile
or smirk at his clever work?
One moment she is running,
the next stuck fast.

        She is an easy catch.
Apollo slows. No need to hurry now.
When he reaches her, her tangled hair
already spreads in laurel leaves.
It's all that's left of her that moves.
Leisurely he plucks the leaves.
It pleases him to bind
their fresh, green shapes into
a circlet for his sweaty brow.
Soon he saunters off,
wearing his victor's wreath,
a cocky crown.

Pasiphaë

Who does not know of the men? Of Icarus, falcon-feathered,
plying his father's fabled wings above the wave froth and aloft
into the sky's wide blue, a boy in a boy's abandon, delivered
from captivity into miraculous flight. Who has not imagined
the sheen off his rigging as he tops the zenith of Mt. Jutkas,
carrying the precarious wax toward the radiant realm of Helios.

And of Daedalus, cunning artificer, peerless builder of the Labyrinth,
then locked inside for its secrets. Who does not marvel at his art,
at his patience, sealing with tedious imbrication the feathers of birds,
at the audacious hazard that made him send forth his son on such
fragile facsimiles? Who does not sorrow for him, heart-stricken
at the boy's sudden career, his pinwheeling plummet to sea?

Minos, too, they know, my husband—the pride-gorged king
and covetous conniver, who dared to swindle a god. When Poseidon
sent his bull from the sea for sacrifice, Minos hid the sacred prize, slew
a lesser one. Then in a god's caprice of vengeance, Poseidon damned,
not Minos, but me, his wife, Pasiphaë—cursed me in a spell
to mate with the bull, then bear the birth thrusts of Minotaurus.

But who now knows of me—Pasiphaë, "the shining one"—and I,
a queen and daughter of Helios, made a pawn in a god's game,
only to be afterward marked by men crafting stories for men
not as victim, but as an exemplum of darkness in women,
of something bestial in the sex, calling me unnatural,
monstrous, the goddess of witchcraft, consort to a horned,

hooved devil. Selene, goddess of the moon, took pity, gave me
sanctuary at the spring of Thalamae, made me oracle in this
ancient place where young men come to sleep in hopes of visions.

In this alembic of prophecies old and to come, who knows what turbulent dreams a wronged woman and the moon will conjure? Remember my name.

The Aphrodite of Knidos

In mid-fourth century BCE, the Athenian sculptor
Praxiteles made the first life-sized, freestanding nude
female statue in the Greco-Roman world.

Praxiteles carves his naked Aphrodite
for the city of Kos. They call it indecent,
but the cannier citizens of Knidos know
a moneymaker when they see one.
They stand her in an open temple
where tourists can come at her from
any side. Men travel great distances
to see this new, indecent thing.
The Aphrodite does not disappoint.

Before her, only men are sculpted naked.
Their bodies are exhibits of power, reveling
in every inch of virility. They hold a discus
or a spear, a lion-skin or severed head.
They invite attention. Whereas the Aphrodite
of Knidos is shown in no great feat
or public moment. Her act is intimate.
She has just stepped from her bath,
one hand holding a robe, the other trying
to hide her nakedness from
someone just offstage.

As Praxiteles intends, her effort does little
to cover the round-fruited breasts, nipples
like the ends of lemons, the shapely limbs
and buttocks, the thighs drawn in
to further shield the v of her groin,
hairless as an egg. A guard is required

to protect her from men who mount her.
One leaves a stain. Another goes mad.
Knidos grows rich.

Two thousand years of western art
will seize on her. From antiquity
to the Vatican to grand estates, from high art
to lawn ornament, scarcely a depiction of
a naked woman will not somehow echo
her face, her body, her pose of being caught
off guard and responding with vulnerability
or shame—a woman who does not want to
be seen, but whose passivity under that stare
was said to be exquisite.

Photograph of a Girl

There are those of whom
it is said the camera loves them,
and the camera of Lewis Carroll,
the reclusive mathematics don
of Oxford, loved young Alice Liddell.
In frame after frame, he posed her—
vivid, elfin Alice—and in each
her child's heart-shaped face,
dark crop of hair and darker eyes
look out, returning gaze for gaze.

Here is six-year-old Alice stretched
on the ground in her white dress
and white anklets, a little sleeping Ophelia;
here the lacy Alice, recumbent on a chaise;
and the Alice he dressed in torn clothes
as The Beggar Maid, picturesque rags
slipping off her shoulders and down
her chest, just past the small button
of her nipple, or Alice-of-the-cherries,
her mouth half parted, for the fruit
he has given her older sister, Lorina,
to dangle above her.

But here is another photograph
of a girl the camera does not love,
nor she the camera. Her look is wooden,
almost drained, her body awkward
against a wall, where she poses full-face
and naked. She is perhaps thirteen.
Her breasts have only begun
to round, the faint shadow between

her thighs scarcely there.
Her picture was lately found
in an obscure French collection.
Its label reads "Lorina Liddell."
Beneath that is written "L. C."

Archivists and experts attest
that the camera, the paper,
the wet collodion process are true
to Carroll's, that advanced facial
mapping techniques match known
pictures of Lorina, that over half
of his hundreds of photos,
at least those not destroyed,
are of little girls.

        What are we to make
of this? Was it him? Is it her?
And is this the end of our speculations,
of our interest here, to see where
she fits in someone else's story?
Whatever we answer, this girl who
confronts us is still *someone*—
someone too young and too used,
with her disquieting stare asking,
where is my story?
Whose looking glass
have I stepped through?

Gentileschi's *Self Portrait as* St. Catherine of Alexandria

In Rome, in 1612, the gifted painter
Artemisia Gentileschi, follower of Caravaggio,
was gagged with painting rags and raped
as she worked. She was seventeen, a virgin.
Her father sued to preserve his honor.
Hers was lost. The trial's surviving transcripts
recount her rapist shouted, "No more painting,"
and record the court's order to crush
her fingers to judge the truth of her testimony.
Her rapist was sentenced to banishment,
but it was Gentileschi who fled the infamy.
Within a year she painted her self-portrait
as St. Catherine, a devout noblewoman,
reputedly skilled in debate. The story echoed
Gentileschi's own in its defiance, vindication,
then torture on an iron-spoked wheel.

The self-portrait as Catherine startles
in its close-cropped intimacy. Everywhere
shadows compete with light. Here she is not
a noblewoman, but a girl. She could be taken
for a servant with her drab turban, loosened hair,
and a dust-red dress with sleeves rolled back
to the elbow. She looks as if she might
lift a pitcher, instead of placing her hand
on the iron of the waiting wheel. Her face
is hectic with emotion, the eyes anguished
and arresting. They look not at, but through
the viewer in a virtuoso rendering of rare
knowledge—the loneliness and remoteness
that becomes the signature of suffering.

Compare the St. Catherine of Caravaggio
in its grand, life-size scale, a cardinal's mistress
for the model. She poses as an elegant lady,
robed in silky hues of ebony and midnight blue.
She half reclines, half kneels on a crimson pillow,
beside the obligatory wheel, where more silk
drapes its menace. She toys with a filigreed dagger,
artfully painted light falling full on the slanting
glance in her curiously unconcerned face.
Even Dürer's woodcut of the saint, for all the genius
in its manic depiction of mayhem and carnage,
does not evoke with the power of Gentileschi
the portrait of a woman who sees what her truth
has cost her and faces it with fated resolve.
And subtle triumph, for close against her body
she holds an upright martyr's palm in her fingers.
Its stem touches her heart and tapers to a point,
like a poised paint brush.

Olympia

She is not what they are expecting, the men
in frock coats and high collars viewing her
at the Paris Salon of 1863, not what they are
expecting at all. Life-size and eye level, reclined
on a frank swell of sheets, wearing only
a ribbon, two earrings, and a falling-off slipper,
she does the unthinkable. She stares back
with an unsurprised look that says—
good God—she is expecting them.

She is no languorous, sidelong Venus,
flesh coyly gauzed in myth, no timorous
nymph with glance averted or sloe-eyed
odalisque. She has disrobed from all
that pretense, that packaging. She is neither
classical nor historical nor anonymous.
She has a name—and they may know it—
Olympia.

Scandal, riot, savaging ensue.
Men call her *an apostle of the ugly,*
a gorilla, a toad—her body *a cadaver.*
Even the soles of her feet repulse—
unclean! malodorous!
And what to make of their unease at
her flower-bearing, black attendant
and that mocking, bedside cat?

They cannot distance themselves enough.
They remove her to the end of the exhibit,
over a doorway, with posted guards.
But she is composed at their discomposure.

She knows her own worth and know theirs,
down to the last centime.
She allowed M. Manet to paint her,
but she is nobody's canvas.

Vermeer's *Girl Reading a Letter at an Open Window*

*After nearly three centuries behind a layer of paint, a naked
Cupid has surfaced in one of the world's best-loved artworks,
drastically altering the background of a quiet, interior scene.*
—*ARTnews*

Vermeer, painter of stopped time, master
of moments that suspend, like a pearl

balancing on a scale, or the interval between
one struck key and the next on a virginal—

see how he holds this girl by her window,
how its ivory light gilds the planes of her face,

catches like tiny ingots on her brow,
falling on the room's half-drawn curtain

and the ripe, rounded fruit spilling from
a basket on a bed. Yet it is the light on

the letter she reads in such solitude
that draws our eye. Though now she is

no longer alone. Experts restored Cupid
to the once empty wall behind her.

He calls for our attention. But he is not
important. We do not need him to tell us

this is a love letter. We have already seen
the sensuous fruit, the bed, the heightened

color in her cheek. Let him have his say,
but he is just an onlooker, a voyeur,

as are we, pushing back the curtain
on her aching privacy, where time stops

in the moment when she knows
what the letter says.

We know it, too, if we look close.
Vermeer paints it for us.

It is the end of love, its possibilities.
He paints it in the other face,

the one we always miss
her reflected face, diminished,

trapped now in the glazing
of the gridded panes, like a lost self,

framed by yet another curtain—scarlet—
like a wound that will not close.

This interior was never quiet.

Giovanni Bellini's *Annunciation,* Diptych, 7 ½' x 6 ½'

Left Panel

What does an angel look like?
Can it be this copper-haired youth
in scarlet sandals who arrives
without ivory drapery or nimbus,
without beams of light or aloft
in celestial air? Bellini's Gabriel
is all action, motion, striding
on foot through the human scale
of a doorway. He enters a room
opulent with color, but his robes are
a cloud of silver and smoke swirling
over the strong set of his shoulders.
He needs them for the charcoal wings
that reach to the floor, so large
they seem not meant for flight at all,
as if sheer weight would hold him,
drag him back from what
he has been sent to do.

Right Panel

Here all is in repose.
Mary kneels beside her pre-dieu,
head inclined to her book.
Unlike Gabriel's dark shades,
a robe of glossy lapis flows
in gleaming folds around her.
Behind her a crimson fall of curtain

draws the eye to her creamy whimple,
the soft, downward gaze in her face.
And here the eye stays.
Time stays.
Nothing happens at all.
For Mary has not looked up.
There is no startle, no wonder.

She has seen no one, heard nothing.
What is this Annunciation
where nothing is announced?
What it is, is simply a girl, Mary,
reading, a girl unaware
of the one whose coming will shatter
the dreaming vessel of her world.
Bellini paints a rare thing—
Mary in the held moment—
not the one of announcement,
but of *before*—before Gabriel
intrudes in his dark wings,
before he hands this reading girl
the martyr's lily and his message,
radiant and brutal.

Spring in the Age of Pandemics

I want to go into the woods,
walk among the old oaks,
the limber pines, run my palm
across the taut bark of beeches.
I want to follow a downward trail,
scuffing through last year's leaves
and the years' before that,
down to the rich floodplain
of a rain-fresh creek, amid drifts
of purple wood nettles,
the blushed cups of spring beauties,
the burgundy votives of trillium
and everywhere the pulse of sun
and new green, to stand in a clearing,
away from the saturation
noise of news, the toll of tragedy
and blame, folly and alarm,
where I can say to whatever,
whomever, may be listening,
I simply want a place
to be without fear, to go
into the world without risk,
to hold another's hand
without concern
and to lie down in peace
with my beloved. Is this
too much to ask,
for anyone?

A Brief Discourse on Healing

Adapted from "Culpeper's Last Legacy: Left & Bequeathed To His Dearest Wife for the Publike Good," 1672

For those in whom thoughts doth trouble the mind,
give to anoint the seam of their head
oil of fleabane mixed with sweet almond.

Let them bathe their head in water
in which strawberry leaves, violet leaves,
flowers, mallows, and other herbs
of such virtue have been steeped.

Let them sleep largely. Provoke them not.
Let them eschew motion of body and exercise,
use quietude and rest.

Let them eat of meats of good juice,
as of pheasants and partridges,
and broth of both.

Let them be merry and pleasant.

Let them drink wine.

April, Black Mountain

The moon, halved like the light
in a parted curtain, still hangs
in the sky, as dawn lengthens
and pales along the ridges,
promising our first clear day.

For days we have been sealed
so deep in clouds we could not even
see rain falling, only a smoky
quilting of mist becoming
water on the windows.

For the first time I understood
what it meant to be *clouded*,
to be obscured, dimmed, cut off.
We, too, closed down, went silent,
shut off from each other.

Now I hear the flutings of birds
and the staccato of a woodpecker
echoing from one mountain over.
The few clouds are like drips of paint
someone has walked through.

It would be easy to make
a sentimental figure here,
say something about renewal,
a bringing forth of light from dark.
But why burden it? I simply say

how it is, what is so, aroused to
the emergence of trout lilies,
windflowers and the ivory stippling
of dogwoods in the understory,
this effortless clarity.

What I Wish for Us

This sun, for instance,
its thrum of light around
the purple crocus spears,
the vocative at the heart
of columbine and bloodroot
leaves like folded palms.
This house, for instance,
that we might go on
in the blue of open-ended time,
this calendar sky, long afternoons
like these and such nights
as stir the surface
of dreaming, part
the mouth in delight.

Boys at Play

You were always better at it,
taking our sons down the long drive
to our rural cul-de-sac at dusk
to watch them ride their bikes
as you sipped your coffee
or a weekend beer, settled in
the old beach chair, your flannel shirt
brushed by the breeze made by
pedaling children as they passed
and passed, raced and banked,
making figure eights, calling
look at me, look at me.

Summers when the leaves were in,
I couldn't see more than flickers
through the green. Winters I could
follow their brilliant caps, the flashes
of their gloves on the handlebars,
as I stayed back in the close,
dinner-ripe house, clanking the plates,
tapping the bread. How tireless

and patient you were, how easily joyed
by the hollow whirr of rubber
and the deliberations of gears,
as you watched, still tall, still wise,
in their road-bound universe.
How long they felt the steadying
of your hand.

Topsail Island

How the children poured out
from the sherbet-colored cottages
and careened down to the sea,
racing the paths through the dunes,
past outcrops of saw grass and sedum,
raising fine sugars of sand
on their candy-wrapper suits
and the small shells of their shoulders,
down to the percussion of water,
to the drowsing umbrellas,
down to where lines of pelicans
stitched the waves
and gulls skated in the sky,
and how we shaded our eyes
at their brightness
as they left us
so easily behind.

Solitaire

My grandfather plays solitaire for hours
with a deck black-edged and creased from
years of steady greasing from his fingers until
the cards seem pliable as a slice of cheese.
He sits with a plywood board on his lap,
dealing out stacks, turning them up,
shifting short rows into longer ones, until
there are none, all the while tidying
and re-tidying the cards.
Then starting again.

I am small enough to fit on the arm
of his chair and watch. He hasn't shaved
and has white spikes on his cheeks. He has
a familiar smell of flannel and Lifebuoy soap.
I don't know the game, so just follow the flow
of his hands in their rhythm, the wuffling
sound of the shuffle, the little accordion
of the bridge, the slight *tic* when a card
is laid. I want him to take me to play
in his workshop, crack beechnuts for me,
or tell me a story about being a boy
and rabbit hunting with his uncles.
He keeps playing. Reshuffles.

That is how I remember it—a restless kid
dropped off on Saturdays at a lonely house
with my grandmother gone. I want him to know
I am there. Though once he made a magic wand
from a dowel and a star cut from balsa wood.
He painted it white and glued on glitter.
So maybe it happened that sometimes

he put his cards down for a moment and
ruffled my hair with a patient hand.
Or maybe I just wished it.

Formal Family Portraits

The photographer posed us in such perfect
arrangements—oval, diamond, fan—
rising up like ivy from the Doric column
of my mother or hovering like spokes
from my father's head. We wore new clothes
and postures retrieved from choir
or assemblies as we knelt or stood
or leaned in, adjusted the angle
of our chins, then turned toward
the umbrellas and tripod
and smiled.

When the proofs came back, they never
looked like us, as we slouched on the couch
sorting through them for those that made us
prettier or taller or slimmer than we were.
If the photographer could have caught us
on a usual day, with my sisters estranged,
me wary, my brother planning escape,
all of us avoiding my mother's hand,
and my father outside on the mower, glad
to be anywhere else—it might have been truer
to how most of our life was lived,
to the time just before or just after
wishing that we were different.

Instead, we framed the wish itself
and hung it up on the wall, where it looked
lifted from a book, the one that said
this is how we tried to look   this is how
we want to be remembered
as those strange people stared back at us,
so fond, so artless, so unlikely.

Next to Last

My mother watches the monitor—
her brother's juddering heart line
rising, sinking. She waits out
each breath. She wants to say,
Bill, get up, stop this, stop it now,
her voice getting short,
a child's annoyance.
Who is there to hear her
when she says, *Billy, be still.*
Be still now.

She does not move as the nurse enters.
How can she leave him behind?
Can't they see it is her own life
stretched there along his?
She would gather it back,
but then what would warm him?

He was the last to know her as the girl
she was, the one who rode with him
in their cart pulled by a goat, who chased
chickens behind the farm that was lost
to the bank, the one in the photo
where they grin in their matching
sailor clothes. Anyone who would have
remembered any of it is gone,
the great-aunts in black, the kind uncles,
the stair-step cousins, their own parents
gone too soon.

In a week, she drives alone to Toledo,
then miles more to a township cemetery
in the middle of nowhere. How can she

leave him to his wife's remote people,
names she doesn't even know?
How will he ever find his way back?
They can't do this, she thinks,
he's only a boy, the one she sees
leaping the creek on a dare.
He could never be still.

After My Maiden Aunt's Funeral

We stand in her small, neat apartment,
holding slips of paper my mother hands us
for writing what we want to take, to be drawn
from a hat. Then my brother and his wife begin
to confer on a cabinet, if it is veneer or not,
while my sister starts to examine the stacking
teak tables and my father pulls a chair up
to the bedroom dresser, picks around in
her marquetry jewelry box. Under a scatter
of WAC pins, he lifts out a garnet ring, asks
no one in particular, "Is this any good?"
Another sister puts an opal earring to her ear,
roots around for the other. She suspects
the home-aides took the best. My mother goes
through clothes, nothing her size or taste.

I write down my grandmother's oak sideboard
with the carved leaf handles. I need time to think
about the piano, the camera by the sunny window
with film still on the roll. Other things are divided
on the spot—plant stands, dessert plates,
two art deco lamps. My practical father takes
the little TV. Piano scores, classical and jazz LPs,
an old golf trophy, are put with things for Goodwill.
I can take my pick from her shelves of books,
watercolors she painted of sailboats and barns
in snow. I say yes to the piano, the camera,
yes to her bedside table in whose meticulous drawer
I find art pens, ink, and sheets of her familiar
stationery next to years of our too-thin letters
to her, in packets tied with ribbons, beside
crisp, long envelopes and the waiting stamps.

An Evening at the Angus Barn

My mother wanted an occasion,
to make a night of it. So the family
drove twenty miles from town to a fancy,
landmark steak house and wine cellar,
built like a sprawling Dutch barn,
with fake silo and hayrick. The interior
was John Wayne western—spurs and tack,
antler chandeliers, leather banquettes.
Piano music from the Wild Turkey Lounge
drifted out over the packed house.
Our black-tie waiter elaborately detailed
the specials, but what one came here for
was beef—sirloin, porterhouse, filet,
New York strip, tournedos, ribs.
My mother selected a wine,
then settled back, ready.

On a crowded, weekend night,
we'd been seated near the door.
My father moved around spaghetti
from the Calves Menu, shivering
from his latest round of chemo.
Then my mother reached across,
took my father's ball cap
from his bald head, said men
don't wear hats in a place like this,
as around us flowed the scurry
of waiters, the scrape of knives
on plates, the murmurous surf
of others' concerns, the chill
of the wide doors opening
and closing.

Portrait of a Marriage

My mother never directly spoke
of my father's last illness, keeping him
to their same routines—the same meals,
the same labored walks through
the neighborhood, the climb
each night to their bedroom.
She never reconciled to

the drugs, the radiation, the falls,
or listened to words like *comfort*
and *hospice*. She simply believed
it would be how she wanted it to be.
And my father let her believe it.
So they went on.

When the last visit to the last doctor
ended, riding home in the car
he said, "There are things we need
to talk about," but it never came.
In a week he was gone.

I think back to when my father
quit smoking. He just stopped
cold turkey. No cutting back,
no patches, no support groups.
In an afternoon he had thrown out
his prized collection of pipes—
the carved briars, the Canadians
the Dublins, down to his beloved,
amber-mellowed meerschaum.

I asked him once if he missed it,
the smoking, ever wanted his pipe.
He said, "Every day."
I wonder if I had asked him
in those long months of decline
if he had ever wanted to die,
he would have answered,
but for her, "Every day."

Losing My Father

I drove all night to the hospital bed
set up in my brother's old bedroom
where my father lay hooked to monitors
and morphine. His eyes were closed,
the blanket to his chin, and the home nurse
dozed in a chair. When I kissed him,
he did not stir, and stroking the thin,
bald skin of his head felt like
touching a doll.

In the morning, I was with my mother
in the kitchen when the nurse came
to tell us my father was near the end.
Startled, my mother said, "Of what?"
In his room, my father lay on his side.
We just stood there stunned, silent,
fixed on his in-drawn breath,
then the slow, shallow exhales
falling away in soft sighs.

An August morning filled the curtains.
I could hear cars going by outside,
a neighbor beginning to mow his grass.
And with it came thoughts of the years
my father had spent tending the lawn,
all the seeding, aerating, mowing, weeding,
all those sprinklers of childhood
and the alarming Snapping Turtles,
then legions of Sears' Craftsmen,
to the unused, deluxe John Deere
in the garage, a splurge
just before he got sick.

My crazy hope that he could hear,
could be comforted by, the neighbor's mower
seemed suddenly irreverent, wrong.
He was beyond hearing.
Then a great onrush of air blew into my chest
and everything inside went small and away.
Outside, the unspeakable ordinary
outrageously carried on.

The Last Time I Saw My Mother

The last time I saw my mother, we spent it
watching reruns on the Golf Channel.
I'd come a long way to see her and the TV
gave us something to talk about.
I'd remark on the players' outfits,
the tidy clapping of the crowd,
while my mother, once a golfer,
would comment on tee shots, fairways,
the slope of the greens. Sometimes
she reached for my hand or let me
brush back her hair the way she liked it.
When I retouched her lipstick, she looked
up at me and smiled. It felt strangely
close, companionable.

When I arrived, she greeted me by name,
knew I was her daughter from North Carolina.
Then as the hours wore on, I reminded her
more often who I was. She wasn't distressed,
she simply marveled each time to learn
I was married, had sons, a profession.
But it grew harder for me to recognize her.
Who was this mild, smiling woman?

My mother was a woman whose furies
and disappointments I had pulled against
as far back as I could remember,
my childhood a series of doors I had
finally closed behind me. Who was she now
to be sweet, to be interested, now
when her mind was snagging, loosening,
when it was too late for any dream

of connection, for time still left. How had I
held on to it this long? I tried to call up
the old angers, the singsong of hurts,
only to feel them slipping away,
becoming the kind of exhaustion
that sometimes must suffice for peace,
for endings, and the beginning
of grieving for us both.

Hard Climb Trail

The December sky is ivory and ash,
a snow sky, but the day is still warm
as we follow the trail down through
a forest of hickories and beech
to a broad creek and bottomland,
each step crackling through seasons
of papery leaves. It's been months
since the geese passed over, sounding
their two-note call I hear as *I want*
I want. And the heron has left.
We watched it rise, slow and graceful,
from the marsh, its wings like
a gray shawl draping its shoulders.
Now only a hawk pair circles and crosses
in tireless, lazy parabolas.

*

The creek is running high from snow-melt
and the tea-colored water winds through
a knit of light and shadow that shimmers like
snakeskin. Stripped of leaves, the complicated
crowns of red oaks stand out in all their
intricacies, stretching up like vessels from
the heart. A solitary water strider twitches
the water and the tremble in the surface
is like a tremble in the surface of memory.

For years we have taken this trail,
early ones with one son or the other
asleep in our arms, and the years when
they ran on ahead, framed in perpetual

photographs, or later, poised on the cusp
of arrowing off into their own lives,
the grown men we still call our children.
Years, too, when we came closed in a caul
of quarrels and estrangements
or raw from the loss of others.

*

The light ends early, but still we linger,
our backs against a deadfall pine, the last
of the sun bringing the scent of your skin
as we drift between fret and dream.
We have branched and forked, bent
and eased, wearing our way into
each other's life like this creek wearing
into its banks, following a course that feels,
on late days like this, more chance
than chart, each current defining
and redefining the last, while the whole
remains strangely makeshift. What was it
we thought we would know by now?
What did we imagine we could take
as certain from these years that seem
to have been but a season?

Tonight the cold, hidden for a day, returns.
The creek will freeze, the marsh decay,
tree limbs ice and split. It is not hard
to find morals in the woods. It is too easy.
Meanings leap on every side, the pattern
of living plain. Time holds us in its span.

As we turn back up the trail,
leaning together as we go, it is not
clarity I want. What I want is to be
in these woods for an afternoon,
with those I love, without need
of comfort, irony or question.

In Sequoia National Forest

The great tree with its cloud-raking crown
stood among firs and lodgepole pines
on a rise near the rim of a cliff.
Fissures from fire and lightning
blackened the length of the trunk.
At the base, its thick, gnarled burls
gripped the earth as if it had
started out life on its knees.

I lay against it, listening to the high
keer keer of the hawks gliding
and banking on the thermals,
weightless above the peaks.
Then a voice was there
in my mind, I swear, as if
from the tree itself, asking,
Do you know what a miracle is?
Then as if in answer,
To be here at all.

And the wind carried the sound
of the voice over the rocks,
over the plunging canyon
and its ribboning river below,
over the molten gold
of the aspens winding along it,
and into the beyond,
and beyond.